Nonprofit Quick Guide™

Beyond Survival: Eight Proven Techniques that Lead to Sustainable Nonprofit Growth

Joanne Oppelt, MHA
Linda Lysakowski, ACFRE

Nonprofit Quick Guide: Beyond Survival: Eight Proven Techniques that Lead to Sustainable Nonprofit Growth

One of the **Nonprofit Quick Guide™** series

Published by Joanne Oppelt Consulting, LLC

ISBN Print Book: 978-1-951978-18-1

13 12 11 10 9 8 7 6 5 4 3 2 1

Printed in the United States of America

JOANNE OPPELT, MHA

Joanne, principal of Joanne Oppelt Consulting, LLC, is a seasoned rainmaker with a distinguished track record of success. During her twenty-five-plus years working in the nonprofit arena, she built or rebuilt successful fundraising departments at every stop, helping her organizations grow capacity and more effectively fulfill their missions.

She has held positions from grant writer to executive director at the nonprofits Community Access Unlimited, Caring Contact: A Listening Community, Family to Family Network of New Jersey, Christian Healthcare Center, March of Dimes Central New Jersey, Prevent Child Abuse New Jersey, and Maternal and Family Health Services. Her extensive background in a variety of work roles and organizations enables her to understand the realities and challenges nonprofit practitioners face–both internally and externally. Her success at every stop positions her to help any nonprofit, whether through her books or consulting practice, turn around its struggling fundraising operations.

Joanne is the author of four books and coauthor of twelve. She has taught at Kean University as an Adjunct Professor in its graduate program. She is also a highly sought-after speaker and presenter.

Joanne holds a master's degree in health administration from Wilkes University, where she graduated with distinction. Her bachelor's degree is in education, with a minor in psychology.

Linda Lysakowski, ACFRE

Linda is one of approximately one hundred professionals worldwide to hold the Advanced Certified Fundraising Executive designation. Linda is the author of ten nonfiction books, a contributing author, co-editor, or coauthor of twenty others. She has also written six books unrelated to the nonprofit world.

Linda has more than thirty years in the development field. She worked for a university and a museum before starting her own consulting firm. In her twenty-seven years as a philanthropic consultant, Linda has managed capital campaigns that have raised more than $50 million, helped hundreds of nonprofit organizations achieve their development goals, and trained more than fifty thousand development professionals in most of the fifty states of the United States as well as Canada, Mexico, Egypt, and Bermuda.

She served on the Association of Fundraising Philanthropy (AFP) Foundation for Philanthropy Board and on the Professional Advancement Division for AFP. She is a past president of the Eastern Pennsylvania and Sierra (Nevada) AFP chapters. She received the Outstanding Fundraiser of the Year award from the Eastern Pennsylvania, Las Vegas, and Sierra (Nevada) chapters of AFP, was honored with the Barbara Marion Award for Outstanding Service to AFP, and received the Lifetime Achievement Award from the Las Vegas AFP chapter.

Linda is a graduate of Alvernia University with majors in banking and finance as well as theology/philosophy and a minor in communications. As a graduate of AFP's Faculty Training Academy, she is a Master Teacher.

Dedication

This book is dedicated to all the executive directors who courageously forge ahead, leading through their missions and wisely managing their nonprofits' resources.

Contents

Chapter One

Technique One: Building Public Trust

You have a cause you believe in and a vision of what can be. Yet, you are trying to meet a tremendous need with scarce resources. Money is in short supply. How do you get over the hump of ever-increasing expenses without a corresponding increase in revenues? Where can you find more people to give? How, exactly, do you become sustainable?

You start with your community. The community provides your nonprofit with clients, donors, staff, board members, volunteers, advocates, vendors, and your reputation. All the things that you need for your nonprofit to succeed. But how do you begin to tap into what the public has to offer? You build up public trust first and show your community, in word and deed, your nonprofit's stated mission, vision, and values in action.

Send Consistent Messages

Consistent messages form public opinion. If you are to establish a good image or overcome a bad one, you must send consistent messages about your organization that are backed up by your actions. One of the most effective ways to articulate and communicate a consistent message about who your nonprofit is and what it stands for is through branding. This means more than just the appeal of your logo. Branding encompasses the totality of the public's experience with your agency.

Visually, what colors do you use to communicate who you are? What about your font? What type of photography best depicts your nonprofit's personality and character? Do you use the colors, fonts, and picture type consistently on your website, letterhead, newsletter masthead, annual reports, and other promotional materials? If you haven't branded your agency to that level, you might want to find a branding expert or firm to help you, either on a paid or volunteer basis.

Branding also includes the words that you use. A messaging playbook, a document outlining your key messages to each of your key constituent groups, is very helpful for getting everyone involved in your nonprofit to communicate the same core messages. It takes work, though. It means that all your internal materials, like your website, strategic plan, communications plan, the case for support, and training materials, have the same words and concepts in them. All the speeches you and your board, staff, and volunteers give need to have the same underlying core words that describe who your nonprofit is and what it stands for do all your press releases, email and text campaigns, social media posts, and advocacy campaigns. The same is true of your fundraising efforts. For best results, do your case for support first, integrating its messages into the messaging playbook. The verbiage in your case for support and your overall agency messaging need to be the same, as do all the fundraising materials derived from your case for support, like grants and appeal letters.

And teach your staff and board to advocate for you and be organizational ambassadors. Teach them the messages to convey and key words to use when they talk about your nonprofit. Staff members see your mission in action every day. Your board members are passionate about your mission. Use their experience and passion to extend your message to the community. Just make sure everyone knows the one core message to send.

Become a Mission Hawk

Your basic messaging, however, is not rooted in how great your nonprofit is. It is rooted in your mission. It is mission impact that motivates people to support your cause, not how great your organization is or how much you need their backing.

Which means choosing to implement and participate in public activities that are related to your mission. Your actions speak louder than your words. So, obviously, engage only in public meetings, committees, and planning groups that support your mission. Maybe not so obvious is the fundraising activities you choose to implement. Fundraising, at its root, is not about raising money. It's about garnering resources to implement mission. Let your mission determine what grants and government contracts you go after. Let mission determine the special events you host. Be exceedingly clear about who your nonprofit is and what it stands for in everything you do.

Communicate Your Vision

If your messaging is all about your mission, your communications are all about motivating people to buy into your vision. Iterate your vision again and again and let people become part of it. Acknowledge public perceptions, whatever they are. And tell the community how you will overcome your hardships and meet your vision. Give the public hope that things will get better. Let them see that your nonprofit is prepared to overcome adverse circumstances and serve the community long into the future.

Live Your Values

During extreme and prolonged stress, nonprofits show their character by the decisions they make in getting through and moving forward. Organizational values may be tested. You must live by your stated values. Which means partnering with other organizations that share your values. And choosing fundraising activities that are consistent with your values. Avoid impropriety and the appearance of impropriety in the tough decisions you face. Again, actions speak louder than words. Show the public that you can be trusted.

If you are just starting your nonprofit or are in a situation where public trust in your nonprofit has eroded, you can build up or get that trust back. Live by your values when faced with hard choices. Choose partners that share your values. Articulate your brand in everything you say and do. Base your messaging on your mission. Choose activities, including fundraising ones, that promote your mission and increase its impact. Teach staff and board to be ambassadors for you. Let the community know who your nonprofit is and what it stands for. Be consistent. Over time, you will establish or restore public trust in your agency.

Wrapping It Up

- ◆ To build up or restore public trust, send consistent messages through your brand, words, and deeds.
- ◆ Pursue organizational activities, including fundraising activities, that promote and implement your mission.
- ◆ Communicate and work to fulfill your agency's vision.
- ◆ Live by your values.

Chapter Two

Technique Two: Building and Maintaining Board and Staff Trust

Your board and staff provide the oversight and operational support you need for your agency to effectively fulfill its mission. As an executive director, you need your staff and board to perform well. Which may not happen during a crisis. How do you build up staff and board confidence in their skills and your leadership, particularly if things are in mayhem?

Building Support from the Front Lines

Workers on the front lines are the most disconnected from leadership. They are the ones farthest away from the top of the organizational chart. They are the ones working with clients. They see directly how a lack of resources affects service delivery. Interacting directly with clients, they get the brunt of client complaints. They also see the growing need they can't meet in the community. In addition, the front lines may have watched as others were laid off and are wondering when it's their turn. They may be highly stressed. And they may show it.

Front line workers need face time with you. Unless you are out there and they see you care, they may begin to form negative feelings toward you, like "leadership doesn't understand," "leadership doesn't care," and "leadership takes care of itself before it takes care of us." If you're not careful, you get an "us" versus "them" attitude, which can lead to a very dangerous dynamic.

To combat negative thoughts, show that you are one of the team. Manage by walking around. Ask your front lines questions about their personal lives and how they're holding up. Acknowledge their feelings. Let them know you understand and care. Give them opportunities for self-care. If you are a large organization and can't get to everyone, go to the key influencers. Word will get around.

You also need to let them know you are still in control despite the chaos they may see. You need to communicate, "Times are hard right now. And we will make it through together. You're still the best of the best. It's why we hired you. Here are our plans for weathering this storm together." And then do what you say. Show that you are a keeper of your word, that you can be trusted.

As frontline workers feel more secure, morale goes up and the workplace atmosphere improves. Which means customer service improves. The overall tenor of the front lines becomes more positive, and the result is reflected in the higher satisfaction of the people you serve. You have begun an upward trend.

Building Support from Management

The hardest part of management is not getting the job done; it's dealing with people. Middle managers are not only dealing with their own fears; they are also dealing with emotions and dissatisfaction of the front lines, all the while showing support for leadership's decisions. Managers try to keep morale up, both among themselves and the front lines. You need them to rally the frontline workers and support your decisions, even if that means negative things like layoffs. Managers certainly have a lot of emotion to deal with–both among their ranks and their subordinates. Your managers may have a need to vent and blow off steam; emotions may be high. And in a prolonged organizational crisis, they may be weary and worn down.

Managers do best when their supervisors realize the emotional complexity of their situations and leadership provides adequate support to help them deal with them. You certainly want to manage them by walking around, in the same way you do with your frontline workers. An open-door policy also helps.

Let your managers know what to expect, both in terms of agency plans and people's possible negative reactions. Help your managers problem-solve the difficult situations they face. During times of stress, their judgment may be clouded. They may be worn down. Listen to them. Acknowledge what they say so they feel they've been heard. And remember, acknowledgment does not mean agreement. It means feeling heard, and thus, supported.

Managers may also have a need to understand the decisions you are making so they can back you up. One way to do this is to have them participate in the decision-making. For example, if you anticipate layoffs, give managers a say in who of their team stays and goes. They know who the outstanding versus run-of-the-mill workers are. Or let them have input on budgeting decisions. Or maybe they can help with the agenda for full staff meetings or help write staff communiques. They know better than anyone else what the troops on the front lines need most. Tap into that knowledge.

Managers must also care for themselves. They may need to be taught self-care. Provide them with opportunities where they can rejuvenate, like time off or flexible scheduling. And lead by example. Show your managers that it is okay to engage in self-care activities. Nothing speaks louder to them than your actions.

Gaining Support from the Board

If you or your nonprofit is in crisis, your board members are probably at a loss and don't know what to do. They may feel helpless, unable to stop what's happening. They may also feel hopeless if things drag on and no one knows when the crisis will end. As a result, they may become controlling to force a positive outcome. Or they may disengage and become hands-off, leaving things up to a strong few. They may direct their negative feelings toward you and become angry or critical, constantly in conflict with you. Or they may be in conflict with one another. Or both.

Whatever you do, you cannot react to their negative feelings. Conflict is normal during times of stress. Your board may need to be taught this. You need to set expectations. Let them know what's normal and typical when organizations are under stress. Let them know both emotionally and operationally. Operationally, tapping into reserves, selling assets, layoffs–this stuff is normal in an extreme, prolonged crisis. We all want to change those trends. But you have to experience the down part first before you move into the upward cycle. A crisis is usually unexpected. Your nonprofit is not failing just because it took an initial hit. It is going to, though, if you don't reverse the trend.

So, focus on survival. Whatever you feel, project confidence. You have a good team in place. You've been through rough times before. You will also get through this one. Emotions will be high–expect decision-making to be more emotional than logical. You must provide the facts and the logic. Be ready to show the board financial plans and numbers. Have several scenarios, including worst-case. You want to involve your finance committee in helping with the projections. You want them to be able to see survival, whatever it looks like. And you want them to communicate their belief in survival to other board members.

Board members need to get to problem-solving. Let them be your partners in keeping morale up and staff feeling appreciated. For example, board members can make calls to staff voicing appreciation for their efforts and loyalty during this crisis. You can also do the same thing with your donors. Take this time to let your donors know how much you appreciate them and their continued support despite difficult economic circumstances. Have your board be the leaders in creating a positive atmosphere and starting that upward emotional trend.

Your board members also need guidance on what you need from them. Don't try to tough it out and go it alone. Tell them what they can do to help you be your best during all this stress. And give them ways to manage their own stress. Don't let the conflict and strong emotions tear you apart. Face the enemy together.

Regaining Trust in Yourself

And don't forget to be kind to yourself. You may begin to doubt yourself and your capabilities. Find your cheerleaders, preferably outside your nonprofit, like coaches or mentors. Engage in self-care. Take care that you remain in a positive state so that you can move your nonprofit forward. You are important. Do what you have to do to thrive.

Spend some face time with your staff. Take a personal interest in them. Tell them what to expect. Acknowledge the complex emotional situations your managers face. Support them. Listen to them. Help them problem-solve. Give them input into the decision-making. Expect conflict with your board. Let the board know what to expect, both emotionally and operationally. Give them tools for handling it. Don't react to negative feelings. Plan for several financial scenarios. Let your finance committee communicate confidence in the future. Tell your board what you need from them to succeed. Surround yourself with your cheerleaders. Know that you and your team will face whatever happens together. And, over time, you will survive and thrive.

Wrapping It Up

- ◆ Be visible to your frontline workers and let them know you care about them.
- ◆ Be seen as part of the team.
- ◆ Assert your leadership to assure staff that you have control of the chaos.
- ◆ Understand the effects of stress and teach your team how to deal with it.
- ◆ Implement participatory decision-making methods.
- ◆ Engage in self-care and help your staff and board do the same.

Chapter Three

Technique Three: Building Up Your Finances

Every nonprofit I know has experienced some kind of negative financial impact at some point in its existence. If the agency is just starting, there is no money. If the agency has been in existence for a while, maybe regulations became stricter, driving up compliance costs. Maybe fundraising events never got off the ground or were canceled due to a widespread community disaster, forcing overall revenues to decline. Perhaps the market collapsed, resulting in fewer individual donations because so many people are out of work or fewer grant awards because market returns were so poor. Not hiring staff or downsizing may be possibilities. Organizational wealth is nonexistent or may be decreasing as nonprofits tap into their reserves, if they have them, and sell off assets. How do you establish or rebuild your organization's finances after such a hard hit?

Assess Your Current Situation

It's common sense: you have to start where you are right now if you want to go somewhere. And just where is that? Not where you hoped you would be, not where you want to be at the moment, but an honest assessment of where you are now–warts and all. Look at data from the past year that tells you where you are now, then decide what you can realistically expect in the upcoming year. If you are just starting out, analyze market and giving trends to get an idea of what you can expect. Emphasis on the word *realistic*. Set achievable goals and let success breed success, no matter how small that first successful step is. Start small. Crawl, then walk, then run.

Analyze Internal Financial Data

You will want to look at a year's worth of internal monthly financial reports. Analyze your revenue trends and associate each rise or dip with your agency's actions in response to the declining fundraising income. What worked? What didn't work? You might want to do more of what worked in this coming year and not do what didn't work, no matter how beloved that activity is. Because your viability is at stake. You just cannot afford to lose money.

If you have no data, comb similar organizations' IRS Form 990s to see how they fared. You can find 990s on GuideStar at https://www.guidestar.org, or you can ask for them directly from the nonprofits themselves. And find a trusted mentor in the field who can share with you their agency's financial journey and guide you in navigating your own.

Account for Total Costs

When you look at your fundraising revenues, look at them at the micro-level. And account for total costs, not just direct costs. For example, how much money do your events make after you factor in direct costs, staff time, and general and administrative expenses? Most nonprofits lose money on their events after accounting for total costs. What is your event net income, really? If it's not working for you financially, you need to make a change.

Evaluate Economic Trends

In addition to internal financial trends, you need to account for external economic trends. What is the environment you operate in? For example, you need to know that foundation funding is more competitive than ever. And that people are Zoomed-out with events. And that while some individuals will not be able to donate this year, others will still give, maybe give more. You may want to grow exponentially, but what really is realistic given the current state of affairs?

Account for Organizational History

Ask, too, "What have we been able to achieve in the past?" Again, look at a year's worth of monthly trends. If you have no history, look at other similar agencies. If you raised only $250,000 in fundraising revenues over the past year and budget to raise $500,000 this upcoming year, chances are you will fail. Especially if you've reduced or have no fundraising staff. Or if you have spent time chasing every opportunity that presents itself as possibly bringing in some cash. You must pay attention to your fundraising infrastructure to succeed. About 80 percent of charitable dollars come from individuals. You need a strong case for support to reach them. And decent administrative skills available to keep up with the recordkeeping and stewarding of your donors.

Also, look at your donor retention rate. On average, it costs six times more to acquire a new donor than retain a current one. And nonprofits are generally poor at keeping donors, with an average first-time donor retention rate hovering around just 25 percent. So increasing your donor retention rate may be the most cost-effective thing you can do to improve net income. Run the numbers. See how much of a difference even a slight change in your donor retention rate affects your fundraising revenues. You may be surprised.

Reverse Negative Agency Financial Trends

When starting up or in times of decline, most often, expenses are more than revenues. At least at the start of the curve. You need to reverse the curve so that more revenues are coming in than expenses going out. And how do you do that when you have no control over the greater environment?

Hopefully, you had a few months of operating reserves, assets you could liquefy, or a healthy line of credit. You may have now used up your reserves or maxed out your line of credit. And even though it was difficult, you reduced your overall costs to at least break even. But how do you get ahead?

Budget revenues first. Develop your income projections assuming that revenues will continue in the same pattern you see now. If you set unrealistic expectations, you are setting your organization up for failure. Forecast your revenues based on past performance, not budget deficits you want to fill. Then cut them by 5 percent. You want to budget lower-than-expected revenues to avoid a deficit.

Next, budget your expenses. And budget 5 percent higher than expected expenses. If your net income is negative, cut your expenses. Yes, it may be painful. But you have to reverse your negative financial trend.

Then make sure you have more than a break-even budget. You may need to revisit expenses again and make more hard choices. Your survival is at stake. You need to start budgeting realistically for positive net income to rebuild your reserves and increase your assets.

It may not be pleasant. One of the hardest things Joanne ever had to do as an executive director was cut staff. And, when that didn't totally stop the bleeding, cut more staff. She was thankful she had a mentor to help her through it.

Assess and analyze your current financial situation, including your internal and external trends. Analyze fundraising income at the micro-level, taking care to account for full total costs. Budget for growth; make sure revenues are greater than expenses. As you realize positive net income, build reserves and assets. You'll probably have to make hard decisions. Outside input can help you keep in check. As you ask the community to support you financially, focus on the life-changing experience they can make happen by involving themselves with you. And then watch your nonprofit, albeit more slowly than you want, get out of the financial hole.

Wrapping It Up

◆ Look at external market and internal financial trends and project what is reasonably feasible in the future.

◆ Account for total, not just direct, costs when creating your fundraising budget.

◆ Base decisions partially on past performance.

◆ Budget lower than expected revenues and higher than expected expenses.

◆ Budget for and ensure positive net income, even if you have to make unpleasant decisions.

Chapter Four

Technique Four: Creating a Fundraising Plan That Works

If you want to have money left over after all the bills are paid, set attainable revenue goals and make more money than you spend. But that isn't the whole story. To be the most efficient, you need to budget adequate resources, account for your mission and impact goals, compare the financial return of each activity to one another, and make sure you have a positive cash flow.

Budget Adequate Resources

Fundraisers need basic resources to do their jobs and reach their financial goals. It pays to invest in your fundraising infrastructure.

Donor Management Software

You may be able to track donations in Excel. However, you will not be able to easily pull reports, calculate donor retention and acquisition rates, capture historical and financial trend data, or integrate fundraising and communications campaigns. Make sure to invest in adequate donor management software. The cost of the software more than pays for itself with the time it saves.

Training

Another expense to consider keeping is training. Many free or low-cost online trainings are available, many of them offering additional free or low-cost resources that will leverage your dollars and enhance your team's efforts. You want to invest in tools that will magnify your team's impact. Although you may not be able to keep employee training fully funded, make sure you budget something. Even if it is only staff time to attend free trainings.

Administrative Help

When you budget, it is important to keep some for administrative help, including fundraising support. You may not be able to employ an assistant solely dedicated to fundraising. Still, your development director must have some administrative support, even if it only helps get the mailings out, enter data into the donor database, or with events. Volunteers are an excellent resource for this. Volunteers can help with data entry, copying and compiling grant packages, getting mass mailings out, researching donors, planning and implementing a cultivation event, asking donors to contribute, and recruiting other fundraising volunteers. For a detailed discussion of how you can involve volunteers in fundraising endeavors, see our ***Nonprofit Quick Guide: How to Involve Volunteers in Your Fundraising Program***.

Reserves

You don't always want to be in this position. So, put aside some of your revenues for reserves. No matter how little. Small savings, over time, will add up. Of course, we are assuming that you are budgeting for more than a break-even budget. It is good practice to budget your expenses 5 percent higher than you think they will be and budget revenues 5 percent lower than you think they will be. And still have a budgeted positive net income. I know it's hard. You need the money now. And organizational capacity needs to increase. Well, one way you are growing your organizational capacity is by increasing reserves. It's a balancing game of adding staff, buying equipment, and setting aside some for reserves. Most often, money for reserves is not budgeted. And then there is no money for emergencies. The most financially healthy nonprofits make sure to budget money for reserves.

Building Assets

You also want assets securing your financial position, in case you ever need to borrow. So, make sure you budget and set aside a portion of positive net revenue to increase assets. Like an endowment, rental property, museum artifacts, or something else related to your mission and will increase in value over time. So, build wealth as well as positive net revenue.

Determining Your Revenue Goals

In some nonprofits, the fundraising goal is determined by a budget deficit. Expenses are set first, then committed revenues are put in. The deficit is the fundraising goal for the year. For other nonprofits, the annual fundraising goal is last year's budget increased by whatever percentage. Still other nonprofits are at their wit's end and desperately try anything that promises to make them money.

Where do you want to be revenue-wise? How long will it take you to get there, given your internal capacity and the current economic environment? What is really feasible this year? Be realistic. Base your goals on organizational capacity and history, not on random percentage increases or budget deficits.

Do your revenue budgets before you do your expense budget. That way, operational capacity is in line with income generation capacity. It does you no good to budget unrealistic fundraising income. What you will end up with is failure to meet the budget, staying on a negative net income trend, and getting grief from your board because you are not meeting expectations. It isn't easy standing your ground when you determine realistic fundraising goals, especially if you are trying new things. Like focusing more on donor retention than donor acquisition. Or building up your infrastructure instead of chasing the next idea for money.

Evaluate Your Net Income

Without mission, there is no money, and without money, there is no mission. So, after making sure your fundraising activities are mission-related, the next step is to evaluate them in terms of profitability. Yes, profitability. Nonprofits *can* make a profit. You just need to invest that profit into the mission as opposed to stockholders. In fact, you need to make an overall profit, so your agency has emergency reserves and seed money for new projects. Setting aside a portion of profits is how these things get funded.

So, after looking at mission, the next step is to look at the previous year's fundraising activities and their respective financial performance. What are your revenues and expenses for each activity? Not just your direct expenses, your indirect ones too. Like fundraising staff salaries, database costs, professional memberships, trade publications, and professional development costs. And executive management, accounting, human resources, and IT allocations. And rent, utilities, and office supply allocations. Analyze each fundraising activity–writing grants, making direct appeals, asking for major gifts, bidding on government contracts, executing fundraising events—as if it is a separate business center.

Which ones made you money? You might want to repeat them. Which ones cost you money? Unless you have another reason for doing them, you might want to not do them anymore. Even if it is the favorite activity of the board or staff. The purpose of fundraising is, after all, to raise funds. You need to make money to thrive.

Assess Mission and Impact Attainment

So, after looking at their mission and financial performance, some of your fundraising endeavors may not quite be working for you in the way you want them to. Maybe they are very mission-oriented, but you're losing money. Or, maybe they're making a ton of money and aren't related to your mission at all. Well, there's a third lens you need to look at your fundraising activities through: the impact lens.

For example, how much mission does that grant or government contract enable you to fulfill? Probably a lot. It might be worth it to you to subsidize any losses with other fundraising activities making you money. Or how much community awareness does that gala or walk generate? You might want to keep them and fill them with even more mission orientation.

What are your other organizational impact goals? Do you want to create organizational awareness? Do you want to recruit new donors? Do you want to mobilize your community? Do you want to provide for high-powered networking between government officials and your major donors? Do you want your corporate donors to get to know your clients? Precisely what are your goals in terms of the impact you want to make through that particular fundraising activity? You might choose to give up more tangible high profits for less-tangible high impact.

By the way, there is no right or wrong answer. It all depends on the goals and annual objectives stated in your agency's strategic plan.

Measuring Your Return on Investment

Now that you've looked at each fundraising activity in terms of mission, profit, and impact, you need to compare the performance of the activities to one another. Comparing the activities to one another will help you determine how much time investment to make in each. You have many activities to choose from. You can write grants. You can bid for an upcoming government contract. You can implement another fundraising event. You can help board members cultivate major donors. You can educate a politician about the needs of your clients and the impact legislative policies have on them. You can initiate an email campaign. You can prepare a direct mailing. There is an infinite number of things you can do to raise money.

Are you just starting out and trying to choose which activities will perform best for you? Does your board want to try to do everything but realizes it can't? Or do you want to make a change to your mix of activities but are not quite sure where to focus most of your efforts?

Face it. You and your team, be it staff or volunteers, have limited time. Especially if you are an executive director, part-time fundraiser, or a one-person shop, time is your most precious commodity. The question is not, "How much can I do?" The question is, "What activities can I do more of that will bring me the most return on my investment? How can I shape my mix of fundraising activities so that they are the most profitable they can be?"

Don't only look at straight net income when you are comparing different fundraising activities. Instead, look at net income in terms of the costs of the resources you invest in them. Divide net income by expenses for each fundraising activity. What are your results? Where is your highest return on investment? What activities bring in the most amount of money using the least number of resources?

Maybe writing that extra grant delivers a higher return on investment than implementing that small fundraiser. Maybe you find that soliciting major gifts is your highest return on investment, higher even than writing that grant. Maybe you find your Facebook campaign delivers your highest return on investment. Whatever it is, that's where you focus your resources when you have choices to make.

Build on *Your* Strengths

No nonprofit is exactly like another. Each has its own strengths, weaknesses, and donor needs to meet. Building your fundraising program on your organizational strengths will cost far less to operate than building one on someone else's results. And you will have a happier, more productive staff. Catering to the needs and preferences of your donor base will increase donor retention, saving you donor acquisition costs. And you will have more satisfied donors who will say good things about you and help you attract more donors. So, only do what someone else is doing after you evaluate the fit with your particular circumstances.

Ensure Positive Cash Flow

Finally, go to your monthly organizational budget, plug in your monthly development budget, and make sure you can maintain a positive cash flow without going into debt. Direct mail appeals and special events, in particular, usually cost more than other types of fundraising. Make sure you have enough money to purchase the needed supplies or secure the needed venues up front. Fundraising performance is never guaranteed. A severe snowstorm. A hurricane. A city-wide blackout. A fire. You never know what may affect your fundraising performance. Manage your financial risks. Make sure you have enough cash on hand that you can absorb the financial risks you are taking.

You need to be able to pay the bills. If you don't pay your bills, you will eventually go out of business. And you need to pay your bills without going into debt. You don't want to be financially desperate. Because when agencies start getting desperate about money, they start chasing the dollar instead of the mission. Mission drift starts. Community support declines. Employee morale declines. Or they make appeals out of that sense of desperation that causes potential and current donors to lose trust in them, and funding begins to wane. And the downward cycle has begun.

Linda had an experience with a classic example of mission drift when a client of hers, a drug and alcohol counseling center, became aware of a Federal grant to provide housing for recovering addicts. Having no experience in housing, they decided it was "easy money" and applied for the grant. The bad news is, they got the grant, totally botched the program, and lost the excellent reputation they had for counseling. As a result, they ended up closing their doors.

Long story short: schedule and implement profitable, mission-oriented fundraising activities that make an impact and focus your resources on fundraising activities that will bring you the greatest financial return.

Stick to your mission, even in choosing your fundraising activities. It is mission fulfillment that attracts and retains donors. Build on *your* nonprofit's strengths and donor preferences—not someone else's. Budget adequate resources for your fundraisers to do their jobs efficiently. And create more than a break-even budget, setting aside a portion of the extra funds for rainy day reserves, needed infrastructure, and increasing assets. Think strategically about your fundraising program, rather than basing it on a budget deficit or random percentage increase. Think carefully about how you're going to reach your financial goals.

Wrapping It Up

- ◆ Invest in the tools your fundraisers need to meet their financial goals.
- ◆ Align operational capacity with revenue generation goals.
- ◆ Assess both mission and financial goal attainment, comparing different fundraising activities' return on investment.
- ◆ Build on *your* nonprofit's strengths, not another organization's results.
- ◆ Budget for positive net income and cash flow.

Chapter Five

Technique Five: Changing Your Mindset— Fundraising is *Not* About the Money

If you are a nonprofit professional, you may think you are raising money for operations. After all, without operations, you cannot deliver your services. And your services are what attract clients and participants to your organization. To someone who deals with making sure services are delivered effectively to your clients or participants, money for providing services is what it's all about.

That's great if you are in charge of operations, finance, or program delivery. And utterly wrong if you want to raise money.

Don't Ask for Donations Based on Financial Need

Fundraising is not about the money. It is not financial need that motivates. Asking the donor for money is asking the donor to pay an agency bill. When was the last time paying a bill excited you? Well, it doesn't excite the donor either. Even worse, treating donors like ATM machines offends them. ATM machines are objects. Donors are people.

Put yourself in the shoes of a bill payer. What kind of relationship do you have with your energy supplier? Pretty much none, right? My guess is you do nothing but pay bills and call them when you experience a problem. In fact, you might even complain about them. Is that the kind of relationship you want your donors to have with you?

Mission Motivates

To resonate with donors, you raise money to make an impact on an issue they care about. To fundraise effectively, focus on mission, not meeting expenses or providing services or programs. Money and operations and programs and services are just vehicles to positively impact someone's life. The prospect that their donations can help make a positive impact happen motivates them to give. So, the first thing to remember when you want to raise money is that meeting operational expenses is a problem. Donors don't care about how much your heating and lighting bills are. They care about whether you are changing or saving lives. Instead, talk to your donors about the life-changing experiences that happen because of their donation. Individuals are looking for mission fulfillment. Foundations are looking for mission fulfillment. Businesses are looking for a strong sense of corporate identity, which, for a nonprofit, is its mission. Always, always, always mission first.

When you choose what fundraising channels to implement, ask, "How related to our mission is this activity? Does this activity build on our organizational strengths? Will our donors appreciate this activity?" If you have declining revenues, the natural inclination is to look at what others are doing to raise money and copy their success. But that method chases the money, not the mission. There is nothing wrong with doing the same type of fundraising as others—as long as it will meet *your* goals. And by your goals, I mean meeting your mission, utilizing your team's strengths, and catering to your donors' preferences.

Sticking to your mission means asking and thanking your individual donors for how they impact community needs, not financial needs. It means researching grants with similar missions as opposed to big payouts. It means choosing special events that are designed to fulfill mission just as much as raise money. Does that run or golf tournament or casino night have anything to do with your mission? Always stay true to your mission. Always.

Your Values Count

In addition to your nonprofit's mission, stay true to your nonprofit's organizational values. Is whatever activity in which you are engaging in line with those values? Do you know what your nonprofit's values are? No? Then go to the strategic plan and find out. Do you lack an organizational values statement? Then work with your board and get one. A values statement will help further define your nonprofit's identity. Which is a very good thing. If you don't have a strategic plan, this might be the time to rally the troops and develop one.

A precise identity leads to increased donations. By making your values known and using them as a guide to fundraising, your individual donors will connect with you at a deeper level and, when they are asked to give at a sacrificial level, they are more likely to. Your agency's values can help you determine which foundations to apply to, as well. Are your organizational values compatible with their missions? If they are, the foundation may be worth exploring as a source for funding. If they are not, move on to the next prospect.

What about your business donors and sponsors? Does your organization share values with them? If you do and you have a strong sense of who you are and what you stand for, your nonprofit will be an attractive potential partner to them. Businesses spend millions of dollars defining who they are and what they stand for. It's called branding. It is good for business to establish a strong brand. Strong branding increases corporate profits. The same is true of nonprofits.

Fundraising is not about the money. Don't ask for money. Instead, ask donors to make a significant impact about an issue they care about.

Wrapping It Up

- Don't ask for donations based on financial need. Ask for contributions to make a meaningful impact on an important community need.
- Mission is the prime motivator.
- Living your nonprofit's values will help solidify your agency's identity and appeal to the community.

Chapter Six

Technique Six: Sustaining Your Current Donor Base

When you develop your fundraising plans, make sure one of your goals addresses donor retention. And when you develop a fundraising budget, make sure you have resources allocated to improving your donor retention rate.

What the Numbers Say

According to the Fundraising Effectiveness Project, the average overall nonprofit donor retention is only 46 percent. That means that for every 100 people who give to your nonprofit, 64 will not give again. But it gets worse. The average first-time donor retention rate hovers just around 25 percent. That means that out of every 100 new donors you added this year, 75 not give again. It costs an average of six times more to recruit a new donor than to retain an existing one. Do the math. If your donor retention rate is low, you may find that the most cost-beneficial technique you can use to realize increased revenues is to improve your donor retention rate.

Doing Your Own Calculations

Your overall donor retention rate is calculated by dividing the total number of donors last year by the number of repeat donors this year. For example:

600 repeat donors this year/1,260 donors last year = 47.6 percent

The above example means that for every hundred donors that your nonprofit acquires, 52.4 of them will *not* give again. This means you are recruiting more than half your donor base every year.

To show how improved donor retention affects fundraising results, consider the following example, where raising $50,000 actually results in more net income than raising $100,000.

	Amount Raised	Average cost to Raise	Total Cost to Raise	Final Results
50 percent retained donors	$50,000	$0.20	$10,000	$40,000
50 percent new donors	$50,000	$1.20	$60,000	($10,000)
Total	**$100,000**	-	**$70,000**	**$30,000**
80 percent retained donors	$40,000	$0.20	$8,000	$32,000
20 percent new donors	$10,0000	$1.20	$11,200	($1,200)
Total	**$50,000**	-	**$19,200**	**$30,800**

Thanking Donors

The most important thing you can do to ensure that donors will give to your agency more than once is to thank them. Thank every donor for every contribution within 48 hours of receiving their donation, no matter what size the gift is. Donors are choosing to share their hard-earned dollars with you. They are going without something to give to your organization. They need to be acknowledged and appreciated for that.

And thank them a lot. Market research shows that it takes seven to ten times for a message to be remembered. That means you thank donors in a number of ways over time. Hold a donor appreciation event. Send handwritten client notes. Have your board make thank-you calls. Thank donors in your newsletters. Thank them at public events. Thank them each time you have an opportunity. People appreciate being thanked.

And when you thank them, give them more than a simple thank you for whatever dollar amount they donated. Donors are people looking to impact a community issue they care about. They want to know how their contribution made a difference. Focus on the human improvement they made possible. Show them they are the heroes in making the difference they desire. Let them see the impact they made, so they feel inclined to give again.

Cultivating

The key to retaining a donor is to immediately engage them in your cause and keep them engaged. Donors who are engaged are much more likely to repeat and even increase their donations. For information on how to hold a cultivation event for your donors, see the ***Nonprofit Quick Guide: How to Run a Successful Cultivation Event***.

Individuals

Start engaging them by starting a conversation. Get to know your donors. Let them get to know you and your nonprofit. Ask for feedback about their donor experience. Let them know how meaningful that relationship is to you. Talk to your donors person-to-person, through text, email, and in your social media posts. Communicate, communicate, communicate. Engage your donors in conversation.

Then go beyond conversation. Listen to your donors and respond to them by structuring meaningful experiences for them. Don't assume you know what they want. Ask them what they want. Then give as much of it to them as you can. Whatever it is they want, figure out how to meet the underlying motivation.

Once you start a two-way relationship, continue it. Ask them to do something, like sharing a social media post, attending a community event, signing a petition, making another donation, and asking a neighbor to join them at an event. Take the relationship to the next level. Then thank and thank again. Start the engagement process all over again.

Foundations

Like individuals, relationships with foundations are based on mission fulfillment. Foundations see their donations as a way to fulfill their missions through the nonprofits they fund. The question foundations ask is, "Where will our money best be used to achieve our legal objectives?"

When dealing with foundations, details count. Most likely, your approach will be through writing, either a paper proposal or an online submission. The most common mistakes are the sloppy ones, like errors in name, address, salutation, spelling, grammar, and math. Make sure to proofread your proposals. Project the excellence you will take in managing their money.

And getting a donation from a foundation is just the beginning. The end of the proposal writing process is after the funding ends and all the reports are in. On time. And accurately. If the scope of your project or program changes in any way, communicate with the foundation. Which means you need to implement the grant when you say you will, not nine months into the project when there is little time to realize changes in scope. The key to cultivating relationships with foundations is communicating with them and living up to your side of the agreements.

Businesses

Relationships with businesses are also cultivated based on agreements. After making a donation, a good way to cultivate the relationship is to agree on the next steps. The next step being, "When can I expect to hear from you again?" Better yet, be proactive and tell them when to expect your next call, always asking if that fits into their timeline.

When you report to them, report on the actions you have taken required by the agreement *and* your measures of mission and market performance. Measures of mission performance can include client stories or testimonials, quotes from leaders in your community, or snippets of positive conversations about your organization overheard during community meetings. You could also send the results of a community, or the finding of a client, survey. Measures of market performance include things like how many people you served within their demographic groups, how many new relationships your nonprofits have entered into as a result of the agreement, or how many new inquiries your agency has realized as a result of their donation.

Government

Government funders want to make sure you have successfully implemented the legislation they enacted. The approach is two-pronged: approaching legislators and approaching government staff.

Legislators

Legislators are in office because people's votes put them there. And that is elected officials' primary objective: getting enough votes to stay in office. If you, as a fundraiser, want to get the attention of an elected official, talk about what's in the voters' minds.

You also need to talk about the public's greater good. How do you talk about your mission to legislators about your agency's mission? Do you talk about the plight of your unfortunate clients, or do you talk about the opportunity to improve the community of the people who vote?

Elected officials also need exposure. Do you offer any fundraising or networking events where they can speak to potential voters? What about your communication channels with clients, staff, volunteers, donors, and partner agencies—can you leverage them?

Government Staff

Government employees are responsible for adherence to the rules and regulations surrounding the legislation that funded your nonprofit. The government has particular financial and programmatic restrictions that must be followed. And your agency will, sooner or later, be audited. Understand and be responsive to the needs of government employees. Know and abide by the rules. Welcome their suggestions. Make their lives easier and they will return the favor.

Sustaining your existing donor base is just as important, if not more so, than recruiting new donors. If your donor retention rate is low, one of the most effective things to realize greater net income is to improve your donor retention rate. You improve your donor retention rate by stewarding and cultivating those who give to you. Your cultivation activities will vary by type of donor—individual, foundation, business, or government. All need stewardship and cultivation for you to get ongoing donations.

Wrapping It Up

- ◆ Donor retention is just as important, if not more so, than donor recruitment.
- ◆ Improving your donor retention rate leads to greater net income.
- ◆ The most critical factor in retaining donors is thanking them immediately and often, no matter the size of the gift.
- ◆ Relationships must be cultivated to continue. Cultivate your individual, foundation, business, and government relationships based on their specific needs and motivations.

Chapter Seven

Technique Seven: Bringing New Donors on Board

In the last chapter, we talked about the importance of sustaining your current donor base. In this chapter, we talk about growing your donor base. You do need to grow your donor base, as attrition naturally occurs through death, relocation, and changes in finances, to name a few.

Individuals

The biggest piece of the charitable donation pie is from individuals. According to Giving USA, donations from individuals make up approximately 80 percent of total charitable giving.

Identifying Potential Individual Donors

To identify new potential donors, look at your existing relationships, including board members, staff, and volunteers who are already doing your agency's work. Look at the vendors and business partners who will benefit as you grow. Look at your collaborators. Since they are already supporting your agency or the people you serve in non-financial ways, it is perfectly fine to extend the invitation to contribute financially. They already have a relationship with you and want you to succeed.

Are all the people in the above groups already donors? Then look at their connections. Their friends, family, and colleagues may not be invested in your nonprofit, but they are invested in the relationship with that donor.

After you have recruited potential donors having some connection with your nonprofit or its existing donors, recruit potential donors who don't have a connection to your agency but are interested in your cause. Don't try and connect with just anyone. Try and connect with those people who will take the time to notice you. And this usually means having a good communications campaign. This is why getting your messaging down and integrating fundraising and communications efforts are so important. To be consistent across your organization and build that public trust we talked about in **Chapter One**.

Researching Individual Preferences and Motivations

The easiest ways to research potential individual donors are through community surveys, focus groups, and one-on-one conversations. When you do surveys to the general public, make them short, no more than four or five questions. Time is of the essence. Don't expect people who have no affiliation to your agency to give you a lot of time.

There are numerous ways to conduct public surveys. You can have a running question of the month on social media. You can have a pop-up on your website. You can stand in a crowd and pass them out. You can mail them out with a response mechanism included. You can go door-to-door and ask for feedback. You can buy an email or mailing list and send the survey out. And you can hold cultivation events where this research is utilized. The method you choose depends on your organizational capacity and your agency's investment in the results.

Approaching Potential Individual Donors

Individual donors are looking to impact an issue, not fix a budget. Tell them how they can make an impact through your nonprofit. Tell them their participation is crucial to alleviating the need right now.

To grow your donor base, ask your current donors to forward your email newsletters to their friends, family, and colleagues who may be interested in your nonprofit's mission. Ask them to share posts with their personal and professional networks. Have them re-tweet your Twitter messages. When you do this, don't always be trolling for financial donations. Instead, use these vehicles as a way to engage more people in your mission. Once there is some level of engagement, then ask them to give financially. Build the relationship first.

Foundations

The second-biggest slice of the charitable pie is from foundations. According to the Giving USA report, foundations account for roughly 18 percent of the charitable dollar.

Identifying Potential Foundation Donors

Match your organization's mission and needs to their requirements. Research their 990s to find out about them and how who they give to. 990s can be attained by searching a foundation's website, asking the foundation for them, or visiting a library with a collection of them.

Researching Foundations

Do your research before approaching any foundation. It's public information. Foundations expect you to know it. Start with learning the foundation's mission, interest areas, geographical giving area, and funding range. You can glean all that information from the foundation's 990. It may be worth your while to subscribe to a foundation database that can search 990s by relevant categories, like issue, geographical scope, funding range, and others. Two foundation databases that we have found helpful are the Foundation Directory Online and Foundation Search.

Approaching Foundations

In your interactions, be authentic, honest, and forthright. Your integrity is your biggest asset. And it almost goes without saying, when you interact with foundations, always be courteous and respectful. It's people who answer the phone, read the proposal, make the decisions and report back to their board and the IRS. People who represent foundations need to be acknowledged and validated. It isn't easy giving away money: everybody wants some of it, and all the causes are generally worthy. It's not easy to tell a nonprofit that the foundation can't fund you. Be sensitive to that.

Businesses

Businesses are also part of the charitable giving pie. According to Giving USA 2020, for-profit businesses make up 5 percent of overall charitable giving. We give you the basics here. For a more detailed discussion on developing donor relationships with businesses, see the **Nonprofit Quick Guide: Best-Kept Secrets to Engaging and Retaining Business Donors**.

Identifying Business Donors

In small businesses, you may just approach the owner or manager and ask how to best partner. If you are looking for grant dollars, you will most likely be working with a corporate foundation officer. The best entry point for sponsorships of any kind may be a sales representative. Often, the sales representative will point you to a regional account manager or director. And those contacts are usually marketing professionals. Sometimes you are directed to the community relations or public affairs director. You may also come across the title Corporate Social Responsibility Manager, who is probably responsible for managing the company's employee giving and volunteer programs and the PR around company volunteer efforts.

Researching the Business Community

Your local, regional, and state Chambers of Commerce, Business and Industry chapter, Rotary Club, and other business groups are a good place to start. At the very least, you want to attend their networking events. Corporate networking events are where you get to interact with business executives, get your nonprofit's name out there, and put a face to the name.

For corporate foundations, review the foundation's 990. And abide by the guidelines. Don't try to fit a square peg into a round hole. If you don't fit the guidelines, it's a waste of your time to prepare a proposal that has no chance of funding. And it's a waste of their time to review it.

Also, do your homework regarding industry marketing and training costs. The internet is full of information. Present yourself as someone who does their homework, is thorough, and anticipates negotiations.

Approaching Businesses

To develop a rapport with business professionals, focus on what you have in common. For example, dress in typical business attire when you visit them. Use language, concepts, and words that are familiar to them and easy for them to understand.

Always be honest and straightforward. Be passionate about the partnership. Your genuineness will engender trust. Listen first. And listen more than you talk; find out as much as you can about them so that you can address their specific concerns, problem-solve with them, and come to mutually beneficial solutions. Go with a fair offer. Don't ask for the world. And only promise what you can deliver.

Remember to talk about expectations regarding communication processes and implementation procedures, as well as the deliverables on both sides. In fact, make the methods of delivery part of the agreement. Get agreement on both process and outcome. And make sure you confirm your understanding of whatever next steps, timelines, or deliverables you agreed to. Nonprofits and for-profits speak different languages that are both English. Make sure to confirm your understanding of what was said. For more detailed information on approaching businesses, see the ***Nonprofit Quick Guide: How to Run an Annual Business Campaign***.

Government Representatives

If you get awarded government funding, the mission of your government-funded program is assumed to be the mission described in the legislation. It is assumed that the legislation and the regulations surrounding it are approved by a majority of the voters through their opportunities for public comment. Government representatives are most concerned with the voting constituents they serve.

Identifying Government Representatives

You can identify your elected officials through government websites, directories that list them, or by calling a government office. Top government staff may also be identified in these ways. Government entities try to be as accessible to the public as they can.

Researching Legislation

Since it is legislation that dictates the relationship, it behooves you to know it inside and out. As well as all the rules and regulations surrounding it. Knowing all the rules and regulations associated with any particular governmental funding allocation is easier said than done. First of all, you need to know the legislation that determined the funding. And you need to know the legislation that the law was built on. And the one before that. Sometimes, you need to go back to legislation that is decades old. Then you need to know the regulations surrounding the financial and program operations of the funding. Be prepared to spend a lot of time poring over dry documents.

Approaching Government Representatives

You need to know and speak to legislators' and government staff's values, needs, and motivations. They want to make sure your nonprofit can programmatically and financially handle a governmental contract and that your organization will be around for a while. They will also be interested in the extent of your reach in the community. And they will be interested in data. Back up your claims with data.

You, as a nonprofit, may not be able to lobby for specific candidates or legislation, but you can advocate for your cause and educate your legislators about community issues. And you can educate your community about legislative issues.

Government funding is based on specific legislation. When you talk to government representatives, know that legislation inside and out, including all the rules and regulations surrounding it. You approach businesses based on the type of donation you are looking for. In addition to your mission metrics, you need to know your market metrics when talking to business professionals. You find new foundation funders by researching their 990s and matching their missions to yours. You can identify new individual donors through your existing organizational connections. By approaching potential donors based on their needs and motivations, you will attract their funding, expand your donor base, and realize greater financial sustainability.

Wrapping It Up

◆ Expanding your donor base is crucial to financial growth.

◆ Potential individual donors are motivated by the impact they can make on a community issue important to them.

◆ Potential foundation funders fund you to meet their missions.

◆ Potential business partners are interested in both mission and marketing performance.

◆ Government officials are concerned with the will of the voters and the purpose, rules, and regulations of the legislation allocating the funding.

Chapter Eight

Technique Eight: Creating a Fundraising Culture

We've heard it all before, both as employees and consultants. And sometimes very vehemently.

"My board doesn't give."

"We are not a fundraising board."

"We shouldn't ask our volunteers to give because they already give so much."

"I pay my staff to do a job. They shouldn't be asked to give a portion of their paycheck back."

"Everyone has great ideas, but no one is willing to roll up their sleeves and do the hard work."

Yes, we've heard all these statements. And more. Too many times to count. Unfortunately, what statements like these indicate is a common misunderstanding of fundraising and what it really entails. If you are to see improved financial results and are hearing statements like these, you must work on creating a fundraising culture within your nonprofit.

The Definition of "Fundraising Culture"

Most people think fundraising is asking for money. But, as we saw in **Chapter Five**, the foundation of fundraising is not in asking for money. The foundation of fundraising is in offering a person or institution a way to make a meaningful impact on an issue they care about. A nonprofit embraces a fundraising culture when its people share their passion for the mission with others. They get others to share in their excitement. And they ask people to join them in making a difference in improving the human condition. Notice that I have not mentioned the word money even once in defining what a fundraising culture is. When you ask people to fundraise, you don't ask them to raise funds. Instead, you ask them to become ambassadors for your cause. In fact, you might not want to mention the word fundraising at all since there are so many misconceptions about it.

Getting People to Fundraise with You

To get board members, volunteers, and community partners to fundraise for your cause, make it a team effort. It is not them fundraising for you; it is them fundraising *with* you. You are a team. No one is on this journey alone. We each have different roles we can take. There's no right or wrong way to share your passion for your cause. Anyone involved with your nonprofit can do that.

As the leader of the team, you need to set an example. Which means you need to give at a financial level significant for you. As do your board members. As leaders of the organization, you and your board model how you want the public to interact with you.

Also, teach your board and volunteers, after talking about their passion, how to ask for financial support. At that point, it's not about the money. It's about furthering a cause and making an important impact. It is our experience that a financial donation is almost an addendum to the conversation. In fact, we have seen donors make significant financial contributions before ever getting to the point of being asked.

That's what true fundraising is: getting people so excited about your cause that they want to be part of it and make a donation because they know they can make a difference through your agency. We think it's exciting to witness and be a part of- making a difference in the human condition.

So, tap into their passion for your cause, both your askers and your potential donors. Which means you have to remind your askers of their passion and not get bogged down in all the operational details. That means having your mission take a prominent place in your board meetings and volunteer trainings. Schedule a moment for mission. Have a recipient of your services come to tell the group how their life was changed by interacting with your nonprofit. Or let group members tell the others why they become involved with the agency in the first place. Make your mission real for them again. Remind them of why they do what they do so they can share with those outside the organization and get them excited about joining the team, financially and otherwise.

If You're Just Starting Out

If your nonprofit is new and you are just starting out, begin from day one defining expectations for those who will be involved with you, including fundraising expectations. Plan to have a fundraising culture. Already have fundraising goals and objectives in mind. Write them down. Talk about them. And only recruit people who will help generate organizational support, financial and otherwise, for your cause. You have a tremendous opportunity to create a fundraising culture from the get-go. Take advantage of that opportunity.

If You're Starting Over

It's more difficult if you are starting over. Usually, change happens in response to a crisis of some kind. Because of the crisis, you may be experiencing conflict with others, pushback to new ideas, and lack trust in your leadership. We talked about how to restore trust and support from your board and staff in **Chapter Two**. That's the first step in being able to affect change—regaining trust.

After that, you do the same things as you would if you were just starting out. It's just that the organizational environment is harder to navigate because of the history. Joanne will never forget the time she worked with a nonprofit that was failing financially. In her first board meeting, the board firmly told her they were not a fundraising board. Fundraising was why they hired her. Little did they know that within four years they would be clamoring with ideas of how they could raise money-with their muscle behind it.

How did she do that? She created a fundraising culture without using the word fundraising. She educated them regarding their roles as lead volunteers. She set expectations for them as lead volunteers. She defined all the ways they could fundraise without knowing they were. She tapped into their passions and let it go wild. Then she let them choose how they wanted to spread that passion, financially and otherwise.

Yes, it takes time. So, celebrate the small milestones you reach when you reach them. Success breeds success. Sooner or later, your success will take on its own momentum and explode beyond your dreams.

Linda had a similar experience with a board that not only didn't want to raise funds; they also didn't even understand why the organization needed to raise money. She turned this organization around by creating a strong development committee that led the fundraising charge. As a result, a strong fundraising culture arose because it came from the inside and from the top.

If you want them to fundraise, ask your board members and volunteers to become agency ambassadors and share their passion with others. Also, set the expectation that supporting your agency includes financial support. Don't ask for money, though. Instead, give people the opportunity to make an impact on an issue they care about. Fundraising is not about the money. It is the fulfillment of the mission that motivates and will bring in the donations.

Wrapping It Up

◆ True fundraising is about offering a potential donor a way to make a meaningful impact on an issue they care about.

◆ Fundraising is a team effort.

◆ As a leader, set the example. Model what you want others to do.

◆ Define support to be broader than funding, but still include financial support.

◆ Tap into people's passions and let them be ambassadors for your cause.

◆ Make sure passion for mission reminders are front and center in group meetings.

Chapter Nine

Bringing It All Together

Your journey to sustainability starts with your ability to build and maintain public, board, and staff trust in your nonprofit and leadership. To build or restore trust, know what your nonprofit is about and what it stands for. Send consistent messages to the public and your staff through everything your organization says and does, including the fundraising activities you choose to implement. Build your team and be a visible part of it. Let your team know you care about them while asserting your leadership. At the same time, be vulnerable and let others know what you need. Equip your board and staff with the tools they need to deal with their situations. Engender trust by supporting and empowering others.

To reach a healthy financial position, you must grow your finances. Revenues must outpace expenses for a positive net income. To make sure your revenue budget is in line with your fundraising capacity, set your revenue goals after accounting for organizational history, organizational capacity, and internal and external financial and market trends. Also, take into count the total, not just direct, costs of your fundraising endeavors. Budget wisely, making the hard spending choices if you need to cut expenses. Make sure, though, to invest in the tools your fundraisers need to realize their financial goals. And remember to build on *your* nonprofit's strengths, not someone else's results. Account for all your goals—money, mission, and impact. When choosing financial goals over others, choose the fundraising activities that give you the highest return on your investment. When you do realize positive net income, put aside some for reserves, some for building infrastructure, and some for growing assets. Make sure you use your resources wisely.

Fundraising at its core is not about the money. It is about meeting mission and giving people the opportunity to make a meaningful impact.

When you want to increase donations, don't ask for money. Ask for participation in making an impact.

One effective strategy to realize increased positive net income is to improve your donor retention rate. The higher your donor retention rate, the more money you make with the least effort. One of the most effective ways to keep donors giving is to immediately thank every donor for every donation, no matter the size. After thanking them, cultivate the relationships. Cultivate individual, foundation, business, and government donor relationships based on each one's particular needs and motivations. Give them what they need so they can give you what you need.

To become sustainable, you must also grow. Identify potential new individual donors by mining your existing organizational relationships, foundation funders by matching their mission to yours, corporate givers by who you know, and government officials through government directories and websites. Entice potential new donors to interact with you by approaching them based on their values, needs, and motivations. Individual and foundation donors are motivated by your mission; business donors are interested in both mission and market performance. Legislators are motivated to stay elected and interested in the needs of those who vote. Again, meet their needs so they will more be more likely to support yours.

Create a fundraising culture about offering a potential donor a way to make a meaningful impact on an issue they care about, not about asking for money. Define support to be broader than, but including, financial support. As the leader of the fundraising team, model what you want others to do. Focus on people's passions and teach them how to be ambassadors for your cause. Remind people of why they support you and include mission moments as part of all your group meetings.

Yes, it will take time. Yes, you start small and grow from there. Yes, progress will be slower than you want. But we promise you, if you take this journey and repeat again and again the steps we have outlined, you will have a strong nonprofit that has money left over after all the bills are paid, and assets to rely on when a funding crisis occurs. The extra money is poured back into meeting more mission. Which leads to raising more money. Which is used to meet more mission. With a solid base of assets securing it, sustainability has begun.